"I LOVE NETWORKING"

IVAN MISNER, PH.D.
AND
C. G. COOPER

TABLE OF CONTENTS

CHAPTER 1
STRUGGLING

I sat waiting for my client to arrive. Let me clarify. This was my biggest client…by far. In fact, if it wasn't for his repeat business, I might not have made payroll for my two employees on more than one occasion.

Dusting off the small conference room table with a napkin, I didn't even notice Jim walk through the door.

"You don't have to do that for me, Ken."

I must've jumped in surprise because Jim struggled to stifle a laugh.

"I, uh, it was my turn to clean up the office," I offered lamely. "Have a seat. Can I get you anything?"

"Some water would be great, thanks."

Hurrying to fetch two bottles of water, I passed my bemused office manager. She'd obviously let Jim in the door without warning me.

I wondered silently if she'd have done that if she knew how tight we were on cash. I still ran the finances, and I hoped she had no clue. I'd already dipped into my personal savings to pay her. How much longer could I keep up the juggling act? I tried to force the thought away as I returned to the conference room and handed Jim his water.

"How are things going?" I asked, eager to see how we could do more business together.

"Pretty fantastic. I hope we haven't overwhelmed you with the uptick in orders."

I shook my head emphatically. "No problem. We can handle anything you throw at us," I said, even as I wondered whether we could, in fact, deliver. "What can I help you with? You said it couldn't wait."

Jim nodded and pulled two envelopes out of his coat pocket. He slid them across the table. "One of those is our updated order. I thought I'd bring it by."

I opened the envelope as casually as I could, but my eyes widened at the numbers. The new order was fully twice the size of any previous order. "Looks like business is good."

Jim smiled. "We've been very fortunate. Thanks for helping us along the way."

I nodded and felt my legs shake under the table. It was exciting to get such a large order, but doubt crept in. Could our small company deliver in time? I picked up the second envelope.

"That one is an invitation. I'm part of a local networking group. We're looking to give more business to a company just like yours. I was hoping you'd stop by so I could introduce you to some of my best local contacts."

The thought of more business sounded good. Coming from Jim made it even better. Almost every referral he'd ever given me turned into a sale. I sometimes wondered how he did it.

It was the mention of networking that made me queasy. I'd tried business networking in the past. There were the wasted fees and time spent at networking meetings. Then there was the one and only after-hours young professionals cocktail session I'd attended. I think I talked to one person and spent the rest of the time checking my phone.

Networking was not something I did well. I wasn't a schmoozer. It was about as far out of my comfort zone as singing in front of a stadium full of people.

"Gee, thanks, Jim, but I'm…"

"I know what you're thinking. It wasn't my thing either. What would you say if I told you that over seventy percent of our company revenue came from that one networking group?"

My mouth dropped open, and I snapped my jaw shut as quickly as I could. "You're kidding."

Jim shook his head. "Two years ago I was on the verge of bankruptcy. Now, well, you see how much I'm using your services. So what do you say? Worst case, I'm buying you breakfast and you get to meet more business owners."

I nodded as thoughts spun and nerves frizzle-frazzled. He waited patiently for my response. Jim's company had been a loyal customer for over a year. He'd even stayed with us when we'd delivered an order two days late. I knew him as a straight shooter, someone who wouldn't put a friend in harm's way. Even so, my suspicious nature and fear made me gulp. My mouth felt sandpaper dry and a trickle of sweat slipped down my spine.

Against the screaming fear in my gut, I croaked, "Okay. I'll be there."

NOTES

_____

_____

_____

_____

_____

_____

_____

_____

_____

_____

_____

_____

_____

_____

_____

_____

_____

_____

CHAPTER 2
THE MEETING

I almost didn't have time to worry about the networking meeting with the work that Jim's order had created. Our little team worked overtime to get it done early. One thing my father, a convenience store owner for thirty-five years, had always told me was to 'under promise and over deliver.' It had become sort of a mantra I repeated often to my employees.

When Wednesday morning came, I rose early and took a shower. My wife had already left for the hospital. She was a nurse, and a darn good one.

I mentally ran through my daily routine as I lathered and rinsed. A glob of soap plopped into my eye, and it reminded me of the dreaded meeting starting in less than an hour. *Who schedules a networking meeting so early in the morning?* I thought as the shampoo sting subsided and I shut off the water.

Rushing to put on my work clothes, a pair of pressed khakis and a collared shirt, I decided to skip my morning coffee. My nerves were already in a twist and adding caffeine to the mix would only give me a sour stomach. I grabbed a banana and a stack of business cards as I hurried out the door, wondering what the morning would hold.

+++

Twenty minutes later, I arrived at the upscale restaurant listed on Jim's invitation. There were already a few cars in the parking lot. I looked around to see if anyone was getting out of their car. Nope. All clear.

Taking a deep breath, I stepped into the dew-misted morning. The only sounds were the birds and my thudding heart. I willed myself to relax, but the feeling only got worse as I reached the door. Making an entrance was not one of my gifts. I always imagined walking in with my zipper down, shaving cream on my neck or a coffee stain on my shirt. You might say I was a bit of a worrier.

I checked myself in the mirrored glass and opened the door.

Inside were small signs pointing the way. I followed them and the sounds of laughter. This was it, my last chance to turn back.

Before I could think to go back, a voice called out, "Good morning! You must be Ken."

I looked to my right and realized I'd almost walked by a small welcome table where a middle-aged woman stood with a big smile.

"Uh, yeah. I'm here…"

"I know. You're Jim's guest. Welcome!"

My face must have given away my surprise.

She giggled. "Sorry. We like to know who our visitors are so we can try to get you some business." She waved her hands in the air dramatically. "My apologies. I'm Sharon."

I shook her hand as I tried to square my shoulders and wipe the look of dread from my face.

"Here's your name tag. I'm going take you right through there." She pointed to the next room where all the commotion was coming from. "I think you're really going to like it."

I gulped as she led the way.

The room was filled with what looked like forty people. I was surprised to see the joviality so early in the morning. Jim spotted me as soon as we walked in.

"Hey, Ken! Glad you could make it."

"Thanks for having me," I responded, as convincingly as I could.

"I want to introduce you to some people."

Jim proceeded to take me from group to group and present me to his friends. I was surprised to see three of my customers, but then realized I'd met them through Jim. I started to relax as they did all the work. Everyone asked me about my business and I answered as best I could. Before I knew it, a bell rang. Jim quickly ushered me to grab a plate of food, and then we took our seats.

I looked around the room as I ate and the meeting commenced. The president of the group introduced his leadership team and some others. I couldn't get over how excited everyone seemed. Maybe there was something in the coffee.

The introduction segued into an educational spot about networking and then what they called the members' weekly presentation. I froze. The president, a thin balding accountant with a snappy sense of humor, said visitors would give their presentations after the members. I put my fork down slowly. I'd lost my appetite.

"Don't worry about it," whispered Jim. "Just tell everyone who you are, what you do and what kind of client you're looking for."

I nodded mutely and silently cursed myself for being so naïve. I was trapped. Public speaking was another one of my weaknesses.

Unable to listen to many of the members giving their pitches because of the throbbing in my head, I hastily scribbled a few notes on a piece of paper I found on the table. Name. Company. Client.

I tried to focus on what people were saying. They seemed to have a similar way of delivering their message. I filed it away in preparation for my doomed speech.

"Okay," said the president. "Now that we've heard from our members, if I can have our guests stand up when I call your name. Please tell us who you are, the company you represent, what you do and what kind of customer you're looking for."

I was the third to be called. On the bright side, one of the guys that went before me was so nervous that he knocked down not one, but two glasses of water on his table. Rising when called, I tried to smile as I stuttered through my hastily prepared speech. I have no idea what I said.

I sat down heavily, relief flooding through my body. *Made it.*

"Good job," whispered Jim. "I think you might have some referrals coming your way. I told you our group needed your company."

The thought brightened my mood almost as fast as the relief of being out of the limelight. I sat back and listened to the final parts of the meeting, glad to be through my ordeal. The secretary, or was it treasurer, stood up and gave the statistics for the group. I didn't understand most of what she said until she talked about the closed business that had been passed between members. My ears perked up. I was all about the bottom line. This was it. This was my out. If the numbers stunk, I would politely ask Jim not to invite me again.

"So far this year our group has passed…"

I listened in shock and peered around the room. How could a group of that size generate so much business? It had to be a trick, something to snag new members. But none of the members flinched. In fact, a look of pride settled over their faces. It was like a football team that knew they were good, but didn't flaunt it unless they were on the field. Something pulled at my chest. I wanted what they felt.

The president wrapped up the meeting with, "Visitors, thank you for coming today. We'd love to have you consider applying to be part of our group."

As I started to gather my things and get out of my chair, two members, whom I recognized as Mike and Jesse, stepped up to talk to me.

"Hey, Ken, we were wondering if you could give us a quick rundown of what your company does," said Mike. "Jim speaks very highly of you and suggested we talk to you about a project me and Jesse are working on. We want something very specific. We've tried two other companies, but no one seems to understand what we need."

"What is it I can help you with?" I asked. This was familiar territory for me. I knew my business inside and out. Nerves were gone. I was back. All business.

They explained the dilemma. I asked a few questions to make sure I understood their need. I knew we could help them.

"How about I get you a proposal this afternoon?" I asked.

"That would be excellent!" said Jesse.

We shook hands and exchanged business cards.

"So? What did you think?" Jim asked as we walked toward the exit.

"It's not what I expected."

"How so?" he asked, with a grin.

"Everyone was just so…nice. Nobody tried to sell me anything. Everyone wanted to know about me. Aside from having to give my commercial, it was pretty good. Heck, I might even get some business out of it."

Jim nodded knowingly. "See? And you were so against networking."

He was right. It wasn't anything like I'd experienced before. I was used to networking events where I was on my own, trying to get my business card into as many hands as I could. Most networking groups I'd gone to in the past were a hubbub of face-to-face cold-calling. That morning's meeting was different. It was like a well-rehearsed play. Everyone knew their part. At no time did I feel alone or awkward. They'd made me feel welcome and wanted.

"Hey, I almost forgot. We got your order wrapped up last night," I announced.

Jim smiled and patted me on the shoulder. "I think you're just what this group needs." We shook hands and I headed to my car.

Maybe I need to look into this networking thing, I thought as I pulled out of the parking lot.

PRACTICE

Networking doesn't have to be painful. In fact, if it is, then you're either doing it wrong or you're in the wrong place. If you're serious about growing your business, consider joining a local 'structured' networking group like BNI. Unlike some networking groups, organizations like BNI take the guesswork out of networking. They have a proven system that walks you through how to be a master networker AND grow your business. They're also smaller and less intimidating.

Your homework is to go online and either look for a BNI chapter near you, or do a search with terms like 'networking group Los Angeles' or 'business networking Nashville.'

Get out of your comfort zone and visit a couple groups. Find one that fits your personality. Ask members how the group has helped their business. You may be happily surprised by their answers!

NOTES

NOTES

CHAPTER 3
THE DECISION

I churned out the proposal for Mike and Jesse in record time. Despite my lack of sleep over the past few days, I felt energized. Something about the networking meeting lit a spark in me. I guess I hadn't realized I'd lost it.

Mike called me the following morning and thanked me for the proposal. He had some questions that I answered without missing a beat. At the end of the conversation, he asked me to send over the contract, and that they'd have it back to me before the end of the day. I must've looked like a grinning fool as I set my phone down and leaned back in my chair.

With the order from Jim and the new contract with Mike and Jesse, I'd make payroll for at least two months. I might even be able to pay myself.

+++

The days flew by as I attacked my business with renewed vigor. I cleaned up processes, collected outstanding invoices and called on customers. As I dug into my company, I realized there were things I'd done to sabotage our efforts. It was little things like not following up on proposals or giving excessive discounts. Let's just say that with the weight of the world on my shoulders, my mind hadn't been as sharp as it should've been. I would do better.

In the meantime, I got two calls from other members of Jim's networking group. One I couldn't help, but the other turned into a small order. It wasn't minutes after getting the signed contract that Jim called.

"Hey, Ken! How's it going?"

"Pretty busy around here. Before I forget, I wanted to thank you again for inviting me to your group."

I told him about the deal I'd closed.

"That is fantastic! Anything else I can help you with?"

I hesitated. He was on my list of people to call, but I'd put it off with the excuse that I was too busy. I shook off my timidity and opened my mouth, "I was thinking about maybe…um…I was wondering what you thought about me putting in an application to join your group."

"That would be awesome. I knew from the moment I met you that you'd be a good fit. I already got a call from Mike and Jesse telling me how impressed they were with your proposal. I think they'll be a good customer and advocate."

"Yeah, so what do I need to do now?"

Jim explained the process as I took notes. The group met every week and there was an application and interview process. They wanted committed members. I'd have to draw a little extra from the company's funds for the membership fee, but if the past week was any indication, I'd make my money back in no time.

I thanked Jim again and promised to see him the following Wednesday.

PRACTICE

It's time to make a decision. By now you understand the value of focused networking just like Ken. Remember, in order for networking to work, you have to put in the effort. Networking is not a magic pill that spawns new business overnight. Networking is a commitment.

Networking is more about farming than it is about hunting. It's about developing long-term professional relationships.

Review the groups you've visited. Write down the pros and cons of each and how you think they'll help your business grow. Think about whom you've met, how you can help them and how they could help you. Focus more on the giving than the receiving.

If you're ready, contact the group and tell them you're interested in joining. Welcome to the game!

NOTES

NOTES

NOTES

_____

_____

_____

_____

_____

_____

_____

_____

_____

_____

_____

_____

_____

_____

_____

_____

_____

_____

_____

_____

_____

CHAPTER 4
THE COMMITTEE

Thankfully my nerves were only fifty-percent as frazzled as they'd been the week before. It had been a productive Monday and Tuesday. We were on a roll. I was energized and so was my little team.

I was a happy man walking into the networking meeting on Wednesday morning. Once again, the ever-smiling Sharon greeted me at the door.

"I heard you put in an application, Ken. That's great!" She beamed.

"Yeah, I hope they take it easy on me during the interview."

Sharon waved her hand like she was shooing a fly on its way. I stuck on my nametag and stepped into the meeting space.

The session was conducted almost identically to the week before. They obviously had the system down. With my nerves somewhat at bay, and my presentation prepared, I was able to concentrate more on what people were saying.

There were a wide variety of professions assembled, and by the time the members were halfway through their commercials, I remembered what Jim had told me. The group rules only allowed one seat per profession. That meant that there could only be one plumber or one accountant in the group. I relaxed even more at the thought. It felt like I was about to be in the catbird seat.

I was the first of the six visitors to be called on to stand and give my infomercial. As steadily as I could, I read off my prepared speech. I saw a couple members nodding and jotting notes as I sat down.

The meeting wrapped up precisely on time, and I waited patiently for the Membership Committee to call me in for my interview. I mingled with the people I knew and even stretched my skills by introducing myself to someone I had not yet met. All in all, I was feeling pretty good about myself.

Fifteen minutes later, Jim poked his head in the door. "We're ready for you, Ken."

I followed him into a back room and took the seat at the head of the table when offered by the vice president, who also headed the Membership Committee.

The vice president, a bespectacled gentleman named Phillip who held the financial planning seat in the group, introduced the Membership Committee and told me that the references I'd given on my application had come back with flying colors.

"We also know you've done business with Jim for quite a while, and he has nothing but great things to say about you. All that being said, we want to make sure you're a good fit for our group. Many of us have been members for years and that makes us very proud and protective of our group. We don't let just anyone join."

"I can totally understand that," I said, as beads of sweat formed on my scalp.

"Good. Now, we could quiz you about your background and skill set, but what we really want to know is that you'll be committed to this group. Have you heard our motto?"

I had. They said it repeatedly throughout the meeting. "Giver's Gain?"

"Do you understand what that means?"

"Give before you receive?" I answered.

"That's right," said Phillip. "Of course, we're all here to make more money, but we also believe wholeheartedly in the philosophy of Giver's Gain. If I help you, more than likely, you'll want to help me. Does that make sense?"

"Sure. It's how I've always run my business."

Jim raised his hand, and Phillip nodded for him to speak. "Let me explain why we bring up Giver's Gain. Nine times out of ten, members that end up leaving us disgruntled are the ones that don't take our philosophy to heart. I'm sure everyone around this table can tell you a time or two when they've temporarily forgotten to live by it. I'm guilty of it too. The trick is to keep reminding yourself to give first."

A woman named Kelly, the chiropractor of the group, chimed in. "I know what we're saying seems almost extreme, but it is an eye-opening experience for many people, me being one. When I first joined, it was all about me, me, me. I was so focused on my business that I didn't understand the key was to build relationships, not book more clients. If I built relationships by helping others, the clients would come."

"That brings me to another point," said Phillip. "We want to make sure that you know getting business from the group is not a given. You still have to hold up your end of the deal."

"How do I do that?" I asked.

Phillip slid a single sheet of paper across the table. "This is our Code of Ethics. If and when you're inducted, you'll have to say this aloud along with the rest of our members." He tapped on the paper. "We take these words very seriously. Of course, if someone's professional association has a slightly different standard, like an attorney whose rules might be stricter, their standard supersedes ours."

I nodded and looked down at the Code of Ethics.

CODE OF ETHICS

1. *I will provide the quality of services at the price that I have quoted.*
2. *I will be truthful with the members and their referrals.*
3. *I will build goodwill and trust among the members and their referrals.*
4. *I will take responsibility for following up on the referrals I receive.*

5. *I will live up to the ethical standards of my profession.*

6. *I will display a positive and supportive attitude.*

It sounded exactly like the way I did business.

"Make sense?" Phillip asked.

"Completely."

"Great. Unless anyone has any more questions..." He looked around the table. Everyone shook their heads. "...You'll be hearing from us in a couple days."

I stood up from the table and shook everyone's hands. Jim walked me to the door and left me with a final parting thought, "Good job today. Fingers crossed!"

He turned and walked back into the committee meeting. I left thinking that maybe I wasn't as much of a shoe-in as I'd thought.

PRACTICE

By now you've either joined a networking group or you're pretty close. The oath that Ken was introduced to applies whether you're in a networking group or not. Read them out loud:

1. *I will provide the quality of services at the price that I have quoted.*
2. *I will be truthful with the members and their referrals.*
3. *I will build goodwill and trust among the members and their referrals.*
4. *I will take responsibility for following up on the referrals I receive.*
5. *I will live up to the ethical standards of my profession.*
6. *I will display a positive and supportive attitude.*

These are wonderful words to live and do business by. Take them with you on your journey. Refer to them often.

NOTES

NOTES

CHAPTER 5

THE NAYSAYER

I got a call the next day from Phillip. "Ken, it's official. We'd like to extend an invitation to join our group as a full member."

We chatted for a few minutes and he told me that I'd be inducted the following Wednesday. He also said that Jim had volunteered to be my mentor as I figured out the how the group worked.

"Jim's a poster boy for failure and success in networking. He's the perfect person to show you how to maximize its effectiveness. I've gotta run, but I'll see you next week. Congratulations, Ken!"

"Thanks!"

I put my phone down and a smile crept its way across my face. It was an honor to be admitted into such a popular group, but the fact that Jim had volunteered to mentor me personally...well that really felt good. I wanted my business to be like his. Hopefully he would help me get there.

My office manager walked into my office and said, "Your eleven o'clock is here."

"Is that Barry?"

She nodded with an amused look as I groaned. Barry was one of those customers you always walked on eggshells with. He could be good one month, behind on paying the next, nitpicky on a bad day. Sometime I wished I had the courage to either set him straight or drop him as a client. Unfortunately, my business wasn't strong enough for that yet.

I took a calming breath and asked her to bring him in.

Barry walked in a minute later. "Hey, Ken! How's it going?"

I got out of my chair and shook his hand. "Pretty good. Can't complain."

"Well that's great. Let me tell you how my morning's been..."

Barry proceeded to tell me the latest in the saga of unbelievable stories of this client losing the contract leading to a delay, and on and on. He could talk a rock to sleep, I'm sure.

I listened and tried to pretend like I was really into what he was saying. It wasn't easy. There had to be a punch line coming. There always was with

Barry. I braced for the request for a rush order minus our standard expedite fee, or maybe it was something else.

"So anyway, like I was saying, I'm gonna need this order as soon as you can get it," he finished.

I didn't want or need the headache, but instead of denying his request, I said, "Sure, Barry. We can make it happen."

"Great! I knew you would." He babbled on about how amazing we were, showering me with enough fluff that I could almost taste the feathers and cotton balls.

He stopped midsentence and pointed to my desk. "Hey, is that *The Oath*?" He said "The Oath" like it was some mysterious tome from ancient Sumeria.

"It is. I just joined this networking group--."

Barry didn't let me finish. "The one that meets on Wednesday? Jim, Phillip, all those guys?"

I perked up. "You know them?"

"Of course! I was a member of the group for a while. Things didn't work out."

He'd pricked my curiosity. "Can I ask why?"

Barry mulled the question over. He looked around as if to make sure no one was listening. I unconsciously moved closer.

"Let's just say the goods aren't exactly what's advertised," he said in a grim tone. "Have you been inducted yet?"

I shook my head, suddenly nervous.

"You may want to think twice. I'm not saying it's a bad group, you might just want to sleep on it."

Nodding quietly, I steered the conversation back to his order. Gratefully, he had the paperwork filled out for once. I thanked him for coming in and said I'd call when his shipment arrived.

I closed the door behind him and grabbed my sour stomach. I'd already paid my annual membership dues, and now I was hearing that it might've been a mistake. Did they dupe me?

Rushing past a surprised office manager, I slammed my office door, picked up the phone and dialed Jim's number.

He picked up on the second ring.

"Hey, Ken! What's going on?"

I took a moment to calm my breathing. Jim must have sensed my unease.

"Everything okay?" he asked.

"I don't know…I just wanted to make sure joining your networking group was really a good idea."

"Well, I've already told you my story, and I know you've talked to some other members. Is there anything else I can answer for you?" His tone was soothing.

"I just…I don't want to make a mistake, you know?"

"I understand. Tell you what, why don't you tell me what happened? It sounds like something set your doubts spinning."

He waited patiently for me to answer. I tried to find the words.

"Was a guy named Barry part of your group?" I asked, willing myself not to say it through gritted teeth.

"Yeah. Is he a client of yours?"

"He is."

"Let me guess. He said some things about the group?"

"He did."

Jim actually chuckled. That threw me. "Sorry. Didn't mean to laugh. I've known Barry for a while. I used to do business with him."

"Used to?"

"Yes, he…tell you what. It's almost lunchtime. How about I buy you lunch and explain."

I felt like a sucker, but I said, "Okay."

My fuming had calmed by the time I pulled my late model sedan into the small strip center. Jim was waiting outside the sandwich shop.

"Let's grab a seat," he said and led the way inside.

He didn't speak until we'd ordered our food and sat down. I wasn't hungry.

"I can see you're still upset," Jim said.

I shrugged.

"You want me to tell you about Barry?"

I nodded.

"Good." Jim took a bite of his sandwich, chewed and swallowed before continuing. "Barry joined our group right around the same time I did. Nice guy. Liked to talk."

I grunted.

"Anyway, Barry did pretty well after joining. I think he got business from at least half the people in the group. He runs a service business that's in high demand, so giving him business was easy. After a couple months, we started hearing grumbles from a couple members. I happened to be filling in as treasurer while the sitting treasurer was on maternity leave. The president of the chapter had received two complaints about Barry's service. From what I can remember, he either wasn't delivering on time or he didn't perform up to standard."

That sounded like the Barry I knew. "What did the group do?"

"The vice president was tasked with tactfully confronting Barry about the complaints. Keep in mind that we want everyone to succeed. The system is in place to help new members, not hurt them. The vice president met with Barry and told him. Barry was extremely apologetic. He promised there would be no more incidents and that he'd fix whatever needed fixing."

I was starting to see where the story was headed. My stomach finally settled, and I enjoyed a welcome bite of my Italian sub. All of a sudden I was starved. Jim smiled when he saw me eating.

"Things got better, but not for long. Soon Barry was absent more often than not. He wouldn't return calls. Basically, he broke every rule we have. He didn't renew his membership with the excuse that he had too much business."

I felt like an idiot. I'd actually let Barry pull me in with his lies.

"I'm sorry, Jim."

"For what?"

"I shouldn't have listened to him. I trust you, and today I doubted that trust."

Jim waved the apology away. "Don't worry about it. I'm just glad you called me. A lesser man would have let the worry fester until it turned into something much worse than indecision. I really think you're going to be an important part of our group, Ken. Don't let one naysayer ruin that."

I nodded solemnly and the conversation drifted to happier topics as we finished our meal.

PRACTICE

There will always be naysayers in your life. The question isn't whether they exist; it's whether you'll actually listen to them.

As we've mentioned before, networking takes work. Not everyone will put forth the effort needed to succeed.

Here's your practice: understand that there will be naysayers in your networking future. She may be a disgruntled member or a bitter former member. You'll hear things like, "That didn't work for me," "You shouldn't waste your money," or, "That was a waste of time."

If you've done your due diligence, asked the right questions, gotten feedback from members, you have nothing to worry about. Whether you fail or succeed is up to you. Say the following statement out loud:

My name is (state your name),
and I love networking.

Say it every time you doubt your efforts. Say it every time you meet a naysayer. Say it every time you drag yourself out of bed in the morning wishing you could sleep for one more hour. Use it as your mantra to fend off distraction and doubt. Learn to love networking.

NOTES

NOTES

CHAPTER 6
VCP®

The next Wednesday, two of us were sworn into the group. Somehow I didn't screw up the Code of Ethics as I repeated the lines after the president said them. Raucous applause greeted us into the group, along with handshakes and back slaps.

I took my seat next to Jim and smiled inwardly. It felt right.

After the meeting, I stayed behind with Jim. He said he wanted to start my networking mentorship. By that time, I was extremely eager to learn. I'd gotten another order a day earlier from one of Jim referrals. I was feeling pretty good about my prospects.

"Today I wanted to talk to you about VCP," Jim said, extracting a yellow pad from his briefcase.

"What's that?"

"VCP stands for Visibility, Credibility and Profitability. It's kind of a ladder you want to climb."

I looked down at the yellow pad as Jim wrote Visibility, Credibility and Profitability from left to right across the top of the sheet. He then drew a long vertical line between each one to make three columns.

"When you first meet someone you want to do business with, how well do you know them?"

"Uh, not very well?"

"Right. So what you're saying is that you're a stranger to one another, correct?"

"Yes."

Jim circled the word Visibility. "We all start at the Visibility stage. As a business owner, you want people to know that you exist. Once they know your business exists, and can place you by name, you have gained Visibility with them. You with me so far?"

I nodded.

Jim moved his pen over and circled Credibility. "The next step is Credibility. What do you think that means?"

"I guess that means that someone thinks you're an honest person, credible, and they'd likely do business with you."

"Exactly. When you hit the Credibility level with members of this group, it means they're now open to giving you business and referrals. They find you trustworthy and are willing to put their name on the line to send you business."

"So you're saying that until I have credibility, I won't get business?"

"Pretty much. Think about it. Would you do business with someone you didn't trust?"

"No."

"There are exceptions, of course, but for the most part people do business or buy products with a brand they recognize as being credible. The last state is Profitability, which means you've not only busted through the trust barrier, but you're a go-to person for referrals. In Profitability, your worth to your referral partner is high. You are an important part of their world. This may not just relate to business and referrals. It often encompasses your personal lives as well. Make sense?"

I nodded as I watched him write names in each of the three columns.

"I've been a member of this group for three years. During that time, I've established some very strong working relationships. What I'm doing now," Jim nodded toward the paper, "is writing down where each member of our group ranks on my VCP® ladder. Remember, this group is my sales force. If I establish trusted rapport with them, they sell me to their friends, family and clients."

I'd never thought of the networking group being my sales force, but it made sense. They multiplied my ability to connect with potential customers. It was like having salespeople out in the field drumming up business.

I was surprised to see that most of the names Jim had written were under the Credibility column. There were a couple, including me, in the Visibility column, and a handful under Profitability. I asked him why that was.

"These members under Visibility are fairly new. I haven't yet had the time to develop the relationships."

"I feel bad that I'm in that column. After all the business you've brought me, surely…"

Jim waved the thought away. "You didn't know any better. This is where you learn how to help me. Don't worry. I'm patient." He smiled to reassure me. I made a mental note to be on the lookout for business for Jim. "Now, the people

I listed under Credibility know me, and some are my best friends. That doesn't mean they've become my most profitable relationships, and that's okay. For example, Henry is a plumber. He's one of my best buddies. We love fishing on the rare early afternoon out. However, Henry doesn't often come in contact with people I want to do business with.

"Let's look under my Profitability list. These members make me the most money. I am their go-to service provider for my industry. A lot of referrals I get from them don't even need to be sold. It's like free closed business."

"Kind of like you for me," I said, recognizing instantly what he was explaining.

"Exactly. When I send a referral your way, I always say, 'Ken is the best company in town to help you with what you need.' That's why they're a done deal when they give you a call. You just have to put a shiny red bow on them. That is my favorite kind of referral to give."

"There are different *kinds* of referrals?"

Jim laughed. "We've only just begun."

There was way more to networking than I'd thought. I looked forward to learning and moving into Jim's Profitability column.

PRACTICE

VISIBILITY -----> CREDIBILITY -----> PROFITABILITY

This is one of our favorite exercises. The trick is to be honest with yourself. Don't sugarcoat it. Take out a piece of paper and write VISIBILITY, CREDIBILITY and PROFITABILITY across the top. Now draw lines down to the bottom, creating three columns. We're going to do this twice, so feel free to get another chart prepped.

Rank the members of your networking group in one of the three columns. Here's a quick reminder:

VISIBILITY means they know you and your business exist. They are aware of you. Communication is in its infancy.

CREDIBILITY means the person finds you honest, trustworthy and ready to receive his/her referral. They might have given you at least one referral that turned into business.

PROFITABILTY means that person is a source of recurring referrals. You are their go-to business for whatever you offer. There exists a mutually beneficial relationship.

If you're new to networking, the second VCP® sheet might be more telling since the first sheet could have your entire group lumped under VISIBILITY. Take a look at who the referral sources have been for your business. If you're a real estate agent, is there a mortgage banker that sends you referrals? If you're a chiropractor, is there a physical trainer that sends you clients? Don't list individual customers/clients. Focus on the referral sources or acquaintances that send you business.

The goal of networking is to get more contacts up the ladder and into PROFITABILITY.

NOTES

NOTES

CHAPTER 7

THE FRIENDSHIP FACTOR

I went straight back to the office and did the same thing Jim had done. Reminding myself to be honest, I searched my brain for the sources of my referrals. To my dismay, the left side of the sheet was heavier than my right. Jim was the sole caretaker of the PROFITIBILITY column. I had two contacts listed under CREDIBILITY and fourteen under VISIBILITY. Other than Jim, I hadn't bothered to list the members of my networking group. They didn't know me yet.

Being a numbers guy, I added up rough totals of the business I'd received from each column. Jim's PROFITABILITY column outweighed the rest. What did that tell me? I needed to fill my VCP® columns and earn the right to move my new networking companions up the ladder.

Being the eager student, I called Jim and told him about the results of my VCP® exercise.

"Don't worry," he said. "That's pretty common if you haven't been actively networking. Most businesses are just trying to survive. Heck, when I did my first VCP® analysis I didn't have one person in the Profitability column. You're way ahead of where I was when I started!"

"When can we have our next lesson?" I asked.

"How about tomorrow? We've gotta eat lunch, right?"

"Perfect. My treat."

+++

The next day I was ready. I'd stayed up late working on orders and got home after my wife had gone to bed. Jim's company was keeping us hopping. The excitement only increased when I imagined my own small business attaining the same level of success.

I purposefully got to the Asian bistro fifteen minutes early to make sure the waiter let me pay the bill. Jim was notorious for sneaking the tab. Not this time. I owed him too much and hoped that this would be a tiny step toward repaying his kindness.

To my dismay, Jim had already reserved a booth at the back of the restaurant. He motioned me over, and I knew he'd already tipped off the waiter. Smiling and shaking my head, I walked up to the table and sat down.

"You're here early," he noted with a sly grin.

"Yeah. I was hoping to beat you to the bill for once."

He shrugged as if to say it wasn't a big deal.

"You sounded excited over the phone. Was there something you wanted me to review?" Jim asked.

"The VCP lesson really got me thinking. How can I jump-start the process and build more trusting relationships?"

Jim chuckled. "It's actually easier than you might think. Let me tell you what I did so you don't make the same mistake. When I joined the group, I was in full-on 'GO' mode. My business was struggling, and I was extremely motivated to make more money. I came on a little strong. Every meeting I hounded my new friends about how I could help them with my services. I carried business cards in both pockets and handed them out to the group like I was giving candy on

Halloween. Finally, a veteran member pulled me aside and told me the secret."

At the mention of a secret, I sat up straighter and leaned in. "What was the secret?"

Jim looked around like he was making sure no one was listening, and then in a voice barely above a whisper, he said, "Make friends."

"What?" I really thought I'd misheard.

"I said, make friends."

"That's the secret?"

Jim nodded, grinning and obviously amused at the confused look on my face. "Look, networking isn't about putting your business card in as many hands as you can. That was my mistake. Networking is all about making friends. Let me ask you a question. Would you rather do business with a friend or with a stranger?"

"A friend, of course."

"Why?"

"Because my friends are people I know and trust."

"Ding, ding, ding. You win the prize. Most of the men and women I see failing at networking are those that don't make it personal enough. The saying that we should separate business and personal is total baloney. Ask anyone whether they'd choose to do business with a friend or stranger, and I'll bet the vast majority would pick the friend."

"So why do so many experts talk about keeping business, well, business?" I asked.

"It's a matter of being professional. Doing business with your friends is still business."

It made sense. I could name four vendors who'd been friends either in college or high school.

"What happens when one of your business friends lets you down?" I questioned.

"That's the point exactly. Being professional means delivering on your promises. You have to provide the same level of superior service to your friends as you do to your regular customers. You don't get a free pass. There won't be many friends left if you screw that up."

"Okay. How do I make more friends?"

Before he could answer, the waiter came to take our orders. I was starving and asked for more than I was going to eat. Once he left, Jim continued.

"We have a simple thing called a 1-to-1. It's basically a sit-down like we're having right now. I like to schedule mine for thirty minutes, and no longer than an hour."

"What do you do in a 1-to-1?"

"At first you're just getting to know each other. It's kind of like dating. Where are you from? Do you have a family? Where did you go to school? Stuff like that. It's good to start with the personal first. We are, after all, trying to make new friends. Next, it's on to business. We share what our companies do, and, more importantly, the kind of customers we're looking for," said Jim

"But I thought we already did that in the weekly meeting."

"We do, but our quick weekly presentation isn't long enough to get into the why and how. During a 1-to-1, I like to have a list of examples of my current clients, the types of clients I'm looking for and referral sources I want to meet. When we're that specific, it's a lot easier for our networking partners to give us referrals."

"Isn't that a little nitpicky?"

"Why? Because I'm telling you *exactly* who I want to do business with? No. It's important to spell it out. Your networking partners will want that. Don't let them guess. If they're looking to bring you referrals, they need to know that you want to talk to businesses with up to ten employees or families who've just moved to the area. That's a lot better than saying, 'I want anyone you know who needs my service.' It may sound counter-intuitive, but instead of asking for everything under the sun, it's better to zoom in and be laser-specific. What if they don't completely understand what you do? Then you don't get anything."

It was a bit of a hurdle to wrap my brain around the concept. I was so used to asking for any and all business. As I came to the realization that I'd hindered my efforts by being too vague, the waiter brought our order. My eyes widened when I saw the huge plate of food he sat in front of me.

"I hope you're hungry," laughed Jim.

I nodded and attacked the noodles as Jim continued the lesson.

"It's important to have a 1-to-1 with every member of our group as soon as you can. Start with the members who you think would be prime referral sources. When you have enough 1-to-1s, you'll know the personalities of the group. That's when you can really connect on a higher level of trust."

"How much time does that take?" I asked, already knowing that my daily allotment of time was limited.

Jim shrugged. "It depends. I know how busy you are. That's why it will be vitally important to have a focused approach to this. But let me remind you, focused does not mean robotic, and I'm not saying you should just go through the motions. You want to connect with your networking partners on a deeper level. Remember, you're building friendships first and business later."

"I think I can do that."

"I know you can. Now, let me tell you who I think you should start with."

PRACTICE

If you're new to networking, or rekindling your fire, take a fresh look at how you're doing it. Networking is all about making friends. Imagine what you could do if you had a core group of great friends that brought you business on a consistent basis.

Here's your next assignment: make a list of the next ten 1-to-1s from within your networking group. Stagger them out over the next two to three weeks, depending on how much time you have. Reach out to those ten people and see when they have time to meet. Suggest at least two times and a location. Make it easy for them to say yes.

Be prepared when you show up for your 1-to 1s. Have your personal and business bio along with two lists, your last ten customers and the kinds of referrals you're looking for. It may also be helpful to mention the referrals you <u>don't</u> want. Sometimes those are easier to remember.

Always keep in mind that it's not all about business. Have fun. Smile. Enjoy the time you spend on your 1-to-1s. Finding out about the other person as an individual is important. Get to know them and their family, as well as the business side of your relationship, and you'll become that much closer.

NOTES

NOTES

CHAPTER 8
LEADS VS. REFERRALS

J im talked about some of his favorite 1-to-1s and I laughed as I listened. He made it fun, and that gave me hope. I liked the idea of spending time face-to-face with my fellow networkers. It was easier for me than mingling in a crowded room.

"Okay. We've talked about VCP®, making friends, 1-to-1s…the next lesson won't take long. Tell me, what's the difference between a lead and a referral?" Jim asked.

"I don't really know. I kinda thought they were the same thing."

"Let me ask you another way. If you're looking for new business, would you rather I gave you someone's name and phone number or introduced you over lunch?"

"Over lunch."

"That's the difference between a lead and a referral: warmth. A lead is simply data, nothing you can't get from the Internet. That person is a stranger. When I add the warmth component, it turns into a referral. As business owners, we want referrals, not leads. Let me tell you about another one of my mistakes. Like I mentioned before, when I started networking, I was pretty gung-ho. Going on all cylinders, as they say. I was on a mission to impress the group. So what did I do? I walked in one Wednesday morning with a print out of all my clients along with their contact information. I'd made five copies. I ceremoniously gave them to the five lucky winners I'd chosen. Their looks said it all. They were not impressed and probably amused. I asked one of them why. You know what he told me?"

"What?"

"In a very non-condescending way, he told me that he could just as easily get a list of random people and call them. I remember saying, 'But these are my clients.' He smiled and asked me what made my client any less a stranger than a name picked out of the phone book. I didn't have an answer. He was right. He explained how I could turn the list into something positive. Rather than give the group a list of numbers, it was much more effective to take the time to call my clients and personally introduce them to my networking partners."

"But don't some businesses want leads?"

"Sure, but don't you think they should be asking for warm referrals instead? Which call would you take? The one from a company you don't know or a call that you're expecting?"

"The one I'm expecting," I said, the explanation finally getting through my thick head.

"Of course! Just like it's important to network with friends, your clients and customers want to do business with people they know, or at least someone they feel comfortable using. When you give a referral, you are giving your stamp of approval to that person. You're saying that you're willing to put your reputation on the line to refer them business. That's why it's so important to network with people who you know will live up to your expectations."

"I guess I'd never thought about it that way before. It's kind of like vetting someone or doing a background check. I'm embarrassed to say that I've already had my office manager print off our client list. I was going to give it to you."

Jim laughed. "That just means great minds think alike! Don't forget that I made that mistake first!"

I laughed along with him as I thought ahead to the warm referrals I could give to my networking group.

PRACTICE

Remember the philosophy of Giver's Gain®? It works perfectly for referrals. As a networker, you want to give the warmest referrals you can.

Make a list of your current clients. See whom you'd feel comfortable referring to one of the members of your networking group. Make the introduction personal. Try to avoid sending a simple email. Make it red hot by initiating a conference call or going out to lunch with your referral and your networking partner. It may take extra time, but it will be time well spent. Both parties will appreciate your thoughtfulness.

NOTES

NOTES

NOTES

_____

_____

_____

_____

_____

_____

_____

_____

_____

_____

_____

_____

_____

_____

_____

_____

_____

_____

_____

_____

CHAPTER 9
PUTTING IT ALL TOGETHER

I hit a few bumps along the way, but I spent the next month doing just what Jim said: making friends. I couldn't wait for Wednesday morning and the excitement of spending time with my group of motivated salespeople.

I was getting into a routine with my 1-to-1s by taking Jim's advice and scheduling them during my lunch hour. Rather than eating behind my desk, I got to network and build relationships. It also came with the added bonus of getting me out of the office.

My employees noticed the change in attitude with comments like, "You've got so much energy," and, "It's great to see you smiling." Even though we'd never talked about the hard times, they'd known it by my demeanor. I prided myself in hiding my feelings to keep the ship running straight, but I'd obviously let the façade slip. The ship was slowly getting back on course.

I liked the new me. Energy surrounded my activities. I had a purpose again. On the one hand, I loved the aspect of giving back to my networking partners, and on the other, I enjoyed the business that started to trickle in. I was on a new path and so was my company.

Jim showed me how to track the referrals I gave and the referrals I received. "It's important to know where your business comes from," he said.

It made me realize that I'd never done the same with my company. Right away I sat down with my office manager and we devised a system for categorizing every new customer that came in. The afternoon exercise opened my eyes to the revenue I was already generating from my networking group. Sure, Jim was the majority of that number, but if I could develop even one more relationship to the same level, we could hire a new employee!

I showed my team how to use the system and gave them a rundown of my referral partners. Some of them they'd already met. My office manager said it would make things a lot easier because our clients were always asking what vendor we used for this or that service. I'd unconsciously found another way to funnel referrals into my networking group.

Two months into my networking adventure, I hired a new employee. I was working too many hours, and the orders kept piling up. The move was probably long overdue, but I'd waited to hit my target monthly revenue so it wouldn't hurt our bottom line. Every week I'd reviewed incoming orders, and I found that our existing clients were also paying us more. I asked my office manager why she thought that was, and she said, "It's you, Ken. We're not the only ones who've noticed the change. Our clients are happy about it, too."

The compliment humbled me. I vowed never to make the same mistake again. A company owner's attitude affects so much. I wondered how much business I'd lost because of my poor disposition.

After our next networking meeting, I cornered Jim to tell him the good news. "That is fantastic. I knew you could do it."

I was probably bouncing like a kid on a sugar high. "So what do I do next? How do I keep growing?"

Jim smiled at my excitement. "Keep doing what you're doing. Make friends. Help your referral partners. Get creative."

"Is that it?"

"Tell you what. Give me a week or two to wrap up some things on my end, and then we'll talk about advanced networking techniques."

My eyes went wide. "Advanced?"

"Yeah. For now, keep at it. I'm hearing some great things from the other members. You're connecting on a personal level and everyone you've done business with is impressed by your service. Do what I told you. Hone your skills, and then we'll move on and put the icing on the cake. Remember, networking is a marathon, not a sprint. You've had some great success early on, but that could all go away if you let up or fail to deliver."

"Don't worry. I won't let up. Can we go ahead and schedule that lesson?" I stammered, eager to climb further up the mountain.

Jim chuckled, and we compared our calendars to set a time.

I felt like I'd found a whole new world. Who would've ever called me a networker? You know what? I love networking.

NOTES

NOTES

NOTES

_____
_____
_____
_____
_____
_____
_____
_____
_____
_____
_____
_____
_____
_____
_____
_____
_____
_____
_____
_____

Thanks for reading. We hope you enjoyed the story. **If you did, please leave a review.** Your reviews fuel this story's success.

For more information on other books in this series, visit **http://TheMentorCode.com**

Visit author C. G. Cooper at **http://CarlosCooper.com.**

MORE NETWORKING RESOURCES

BNI: With over 160,000 members worldwide, BNI is the largest business networking organization in the world. Last year alone, BNI generated 5.4 million referrals, resulting in $6.5 billion dollars worth of business for its members. We offer members the opportunity to share ideas, contacts, and most importantly, business referrals. For more information, visit **www.BNI.com**.

Referral Institute®: The Referral Institute's vision is to be the world's leader helping entrepreneurs create Referrals For Life®. Creating Referrals For Life® means our clients will be working within communities of like-minded entrepreneurs to:

- Work with the type of people you enjoy
- Eliminate cold calls
- Have the Life style you deserve

Referrals For Life® is not just a marketing technique, it's a life style.

For more information, visit
www.ReferralInstitute.com